Original title:
Swaying with the Palm Trees

Copyright © 2025 Creative Arts Management OÜ
All rights reserved.

Author: Julian Carmichael
ISBN HARDBACK: 978-1-80581-538-9
ISBN PAPERBACK: 978-1-80581-065-0
ISBN EBOOK: 978-1-80581-538-9

Nature's Gentle Rhythm

Waving leaves with no alarm,
While critters try to charm.
The breeze just takes a stroll,
And leaves us giggling whole.

The sun shines down, no shame,
As ants play their silly game.
Grasshoppers leap with flair,
While birds avoid the chair.

A cloud drifts by so sly,
Tickling the sky on high.
Nature's dance is quite a show,
Where laughter's sure to flow.

In the shade we plot and scheme,
To catch that wild ice cream.
With snacks that fly and bounce,
We giggle and we pounce.

Shadows and Dreams

Beneath the branches wide and green,
The shadows hold a funny scene.
A squirrel backflips with some flair,
While dreaming of his lunchtime care.

The butterflies parade with glee,
In costumes that are hard to see.
They dance around in silly spins,
Taking bets on who wins.

The wind whispers jokes, quite absurd,
While frogs croak punchlines unheard.
They ribbit with a perfect rhyme,
As if they've mastered comic time.

In this wild and wacky place,
Laughter beams upon each face.
With shadows stretching far and wide,
Nature's humor is our guide.

Dancing Shadows at Dusk

Beneath the evening's gentle fade,
The shadows twist in parade.
A lizard joins the funky beat,
As crickets tap their tiny feet.

The breeze plays tricks on tangled leaves,
While squirrels plot and scheme like thieves.
The sun dips low, it starts to dance,
As all the creatures take a chance.

Tropical Whirl

Coconuts are falling down,
As monkeys wear their crown.
The parrots chuckle from the top,
While all the tourists flip and flop.

The tides are in a constant spin,
The fish are laughing, let's begin!
With seaweed hats and fins of grace,
Each creature joins the crazy race.

Echoing Through the Canopy

In the trees, a giggle flies,
As butterflies tease with painted sighs.
The branches sway as if to tease,
The laughter drifts upon the breeze.

A sloth drops down with slow delight,
He waves and winks, what a sight!
The echoes bounce from leaf to moss,
"Join the fun or face the loss!"

Nature's Lullaby

Under stars, the wild things croon,
The owls hoot a funky tune.
A raccoon rolls in twinkly lights,
As crickets chirp throughout the nights.

The fireflies blink in silly dance,
While frogs engage in their romance.
Nature hums a tune so bright,
Inviting all to join the night.

A Symphony of the Shoreline

The shells danced to the waves' funky tune,
While crabs played violin under the moon.
Seagulls squawk like flutes, quite out of key,
As fish keep the rhythm, oh what a spree!

The sandcastles wobble in grandeur so tall,
While kids in their shorts run and trip in a sprawl.
A mermaid reclines, sipping soda with flair,
As sun-kissed sunbathers pretend they don't care.

Secrets Held by Swaying Giants

Bamboo whispers secrets they promise to keep,
To flip-flop wearers who nod off in sleep.
Each breeze tells a story, a giggle or two,
As squirrels hold debates on the best nuts to chew.

Beneath a big tree, a raccoon does prance,
While seagulls practice their wildest of dance.
Leaves twinkle with laughter, the sun starts to wink,
As waves poke the shore, too busy to think.

Melodies of the Coastal Breeze

The breeze blows a tune with a hiccup and loop,
As dolphins engage in a synchronized scoop.
Turtles in sunglasses rock out on the shore,
While jellyfish jiggle, behaving quite poor.

Clams keep the beat with a shuffle so smooth,
While crabs form a band with a percussive groove.
The sun beams a spotlight on all of this craze,
As everyone chuckles, lost in the maze.

Fronds in a Celestial Waltz

Leaves twirl like dancers under the sun's soft gaze,
Best friends all around in this comical phase.
A gang of coconuts giggle and roll,
As parrots parlay, what a curious toll!

The tide ebbs and flows with a jester's delight,
While octopuses juggle, an incredible sight.
The clouds form a stage, with laughter anew,
As the shoreline throws a party just for the crew!

Under the Tropical Veil

Beneath the sky so bright and clear,
The leaves bring giggles, loud and near.
They rustle tales of a dancing breeze,
While sunbaked tourists try to freeze.

The coconuts play peek-a-boo,
Rolling away with each wild view.
A monkey swings, a laugh in tow,
As beach umbrellas start to blow.

In the shade, a crab does prance,
Creeping sideways, takes a chance.
With every step, a comical fight,
Who knew the beach could bring such light?

Fronds overhead, they wave and wink,
Teasing sunburns and a drink.
Under this tropical comedy scene,
Life feels like a playful dream.

Leaves that Speak to the Wind

The leaves gossip loudly, oh what a noise,
Sharing secrets of sandcastles and toys.
They giggle at tourists with beach hats wide,
As waves tickle toes with a giggling tide.

A silly seagull goes down the line,
Snatching fries, oh what a crime!
With every flight, they flap and dive,
While locals laugh, oh, how they thrive!

A playful breeze takes hats away,
The tourists chase, much like a ballet.
Fronds twist in glee, what a funny sight,
While sun-kissed folks dance in delight.

Each leaf is a jester, every vine a tease,
Spreading joy with the greatest of ease.
In this vibrant world where laughter grows,
Nature's humor in every blow.

Choreography of Sunlit Fronds

Fronds curtsy low, then twirl with grace,
Offering shade in a sunny embrace.
They shimmy and shake like they own the place,
As folks drink smoothies at a thunderous pace.

The sunbeams flash like disco lights,
Making the palm tops dance all night.
With laughter echoing on breezy trails,
Even the lizards join in the tales.

Their dear choreography, quite the show,
While someone spills juice, oh no, oh no!
Slippery smiles and giggles abound,
As nature spins round, joyfully unbound.

In this tropical theater, all are stars,
Regular traffic, cars and bars.
Yet here in the sun, with fronds twirling free,
Life's silly dance is a joyful spree.

Nature's Lullaby in Green

In the warm embrace of leafy delight,
Nature hums softly, day turns to night.
Breezes whisper secrets of joyful dreams,
While fireflies twinkle like sweet little beams.

A crab in a shell sings a little tune,
Wiggling its claws under the laughing moon.
With every rustle, the leaves quicken pace,
As frogs join the chorus, a lively race.

The coconuts giggle as they drop from above,
Bouncing like children, oh how they shove!
While resting in hammocks, we chuckle anew,
Nature's sweet lullaby makes joy break through.

In this wild symphony, all play their part,
With humor woven in Mother Nature's art.
So come join the laughter under the trees,
For life's but a game, and we hold the keys!

Breeze-kissed Whispers

In the wind, the leaves play tag,
Laughter spills from branches high.
Fronds are giggling, swaying, swish,
As if they're cooking up a wish.

Sunbeams dance on sandy toes,
While coconut dreams start to doze.
Breezes tickle, what a treat,
Palms take selfies, isn't that neat?

Seagulls join with raucous cheer,
Plucking at the friendly sphere.
"Let's surf the waves, let's ride and glide,"
Shouts a crab, with a wink of pride.

At dusk the shadows play a game,
With moonlight cast in a soft frame.
Each palm's got stories, oh so wild,
Like giggles from a playful child.

Dancing Shadows under the Canopy

Under green hats, oh what fun,
Leaves are dancing, one by one.
They wear the heights like fashion crowns,
With roots deep down in sandy towns.

The breeze brings jokes from far-off shores,
As rhinoceros beetles scout for stores.
"Catch me if you can!" cries a playful ant,
While a lizard practices its new dance chant.

Juggling fruit, the monkeys play,
On branches that twist, stretch and sway.
Every tumble met with a cheer,
For even in spills, joy draws near.

Shadows twist, like silly hats,
Painting laughter in the chats.
Under fluorescent light of stars,
Life's a hoot, no matter how far.

Rhythms of the Ocean's Embrace

The tide hums tunes, with a splash so bright,
Seagulls perform in a feathery flight.
Palm leaves shake like they've got the beat,
As sandy feet dance to the heat.

Crabs crab-walk in a funny parade,
While dolphins jump in a glistening charade.
Every splash sends giggles high,
Under the gaze of a watchful sky.

Coconut shells roll past with glee,
While jellyfish twirl like they're crazy and free.
Each wave a tickle, a friendly tease,
Mother Ocean laughs with the greatest of ease.

Starfish wiggle, waving hello,
In a bubbly world where smiles grow.
It's a frolic of creatures, pure delight,
In ocean's embrace, everything feels right.

Serenity's Gentle Motion

Softly rocks the green brigade,
In sunlit chatter, they invade.
Leaves trade tales with the sky so blue,
Of all the fun they've swirled right through.

A picnic of clouds drifts overhead,
While ants form lines, like parties spread.
"Let's conquer the hill!" they say with glee,
While a bumblebee hums a melody.

Barefoot strolls on a pastel shore,
As laughter tumbles and lingers more.
Frolicking critters, a joyous sight,
In gentle motion, all feels right.

The breeze whispers jokes that set hearts aglow,
In nature's embrace, oh how we flow.
With every tickle from the palm's soft hand,
Happiness blooms in this fine land.

Shadows on the Beach

On the sand, I stand so proud,
Waving at tourists, feeling loud.
A flip-flop flies, oh where it goes,
Chasing crabs—oh, what a show!

The sun is bright, I take a seat,
A seagull lands; he wants a treat.
I toss a chip, he looks amused,
That snack was for me—he's so confused!

My shadow's long, it starts to dance,
A jig or two, I take the chance.
Tiny feet join in the fun,
Who knew that shadows could run?

With laughter echoing on the shore,
I do a twist—then hit the floor.
The waves just laugh, they roll and swell,
As I tell tales of this beachy spell.

Rhythm of the Tropics

The sun beats down, I feel the groove,
A dance-off begins, I make my move.
The locals laugh, they cheer me on,
My two left feet, but I'm never gone!

A parrot squawks, he wants to sing,
But I just can't keep up with wing.
He flaps around, I try to keep
The beat, oh no! I start to leap.

The drinks are cold, a fruity mix,
With tiny umbrellas—oh, what a fix!
I raise my glass and take a sip,
The rhythm makes me want to flip.

The night descends, the stars come out,
I'm still dancing, no doubt about.
In this tropical beat, I find the way,
To move and groove till the break of day.

Embrace of the Breeze

A gentle gust, it tickles my nose,
I try to breathe, and it goes—who knows?
In my sunhat, I'm losing control,
It lifts me high, oh what a stroll!

The beach chairs tumble, they roll on by,
As I wave at seagulls—oh, my, oh my!
The breeze just laughs, I'm in a tizzy,
Chasing my hat, oh it's such a busy!

I spot a kite, it climbs so high,
My hat goes up, I let out a sigh.
I dart, I dash, it's a windy race,
The beach folks giggle, what a wild chase!

In the end, with hair askew,
I claim victory—we all knew.
The breeze my partner, we dance in glee,
As sand in my shorts sings, "Just be free!"

Whispering Leaves

The breezy leaves whisper secrets low,
They giggle and jest, it's quite the show.
I lean in close to hear their chat,
But I'm just a human; I'm not a cat!

As they chuckle, I swirl around,
Tripping over roots that grasp the ground.
They tease me on this sunny bluff,
Saying, "Hold on tight! Life's not that tough!"

Some coconuts drop, a plunk on my head,
The leaves roar with laughter—"Time for bed!"
I nurse my bruise, but can't help but grin,
Nature's a hoot, not just my kin!

With a final twirl, I take my leave,
But the leaves will stay, so I believe.
Next time I'm here, I'll shake my tail,
To the whisper of leaves in the summer gale!

Shifting Silhouettes

Under the sun, they dance so bold,
Swinging their arms, stories unfold.
Those leafy fronds, they seem to tease,
While the breeze whispers, 'Do as you please!'

Tall and proud, they twist and bend,
With funny shapes, they seem to send.
A wave to the sky, a wink at the ground,
In this leafy party, laughter is found!

They sway like they're in a goofy race,
Chasing shadows, a wild embrace.
The sun chuckles low, the clouds join in,
In this leafy dance, everyone wins!

With roots deep in laughter, they stand so free,
Nature's jesters, it's quite the spree.
In the lighthearted fun, don't you agree?
Join in the joy, beneath the tall green spree!

Sunlit Canopy Dreams

The canopy's bright with a vibrant zest,
Leaves bounce around, putting humor to test.
They tickle the clouds, send giggles below,
In this sunny realm, there's a funny show!

Twirling around in a dizzy dance,
Each leaf takes turns, it's their funny chance.
They flap and flutter, like they've lost their hat,
What a sight to see, a wild acrobat!

With a rustle and a laugh, they start to plot,
Making shapes and shadows, oh what a thought!
Playing hide and seek with a chirping bird,
In the sunlit dreams, hilarity stirred.

A comical breeze gives a playful shove,
In the canopy's charm, we can't help but love.
As giggles arise from the branches high,
Join the laughter, let your spirit fly!

Waving to the Horizon

Arms stretched wide in a playful cheer,
Reaching for sunsets, oh so near.
They giggle and wave, a merry display,
Greeting the horizon in a fun-filled way!

With every gust, they sway and grin,
No one can tell where the fun begins.
They flirt with the wind, teasing the tide,
In this joyful jest, they refuse to hide!

They chuckle at clouds, who trip on their path,
Making strange shapes, igniting our laugh.
A whimsical breeze spins tales of delight,
Bringing mischief until the night!

On this bright shore, the fun never ends,
As they wave 'hello' to all of their friends.
With laughter so loud, a sound heavenly,
Join the fun, come, dance with glee!

Echoes of the Ocean

The waves crash like laughter, a playful sound,
While the leafy dancers whirl all around.
Echoes of joy in the salty air,
Nature's giggles, without a care!

With stories of fish that tickle and tease,
The sunbeams join in, doing as they please.
Leaves ruffle their edges like a playful chat,
Fun in the tide, can you handle that?

Gulls swoop down for a wacky show,
While the trees do their thing, with a cheeky glow.
Each echo a chorus of life's bright jest,
In this wild ruckus, we simply feel blessed!

With every pulse of this vibrant strand,
We join the fun, hand in leafy hand.
In the echoes of laughter, let's sing along,
In this wild ocean dance, we all belong!

Dappled Light and Breeze

Beneath the dappled light we lounge,
The wind plays tricks, it loves to scrounge.
A coconut drops, it rolls away,
The beach ball laughs, let's play today!

With sun hats askew, we dance in cheer,
A seagull squawks, it won't come near.
We chase our dreams like sand on toes,
In this quirky place, anything goes!

We stumble, we tumble, in pure delight,
Chasing shadows 'til fall turns night.
The ocean's giggle joins our play,
As the world spins round in a merry ballet!

So grab your shades and join the fun,
Under the sky, we all are one.
With gleeful hearts that leap so free,
In this whimsical dance, just you and me!

The Canopy's Secret Song

Up high in the canopy, a tune is found,
Birds perform their antics, oh what a sound!
A squirrel's cheeky wink gives us a laugh,
As he hoards acorns, drawing his own craft.

The leaves sway gently to secrets untold,
Whispering tales of the brave and bold.
In every rustle, a chuckle is heard,
As nature herself joins in this absurd!

Sunbeams flicker like playful sprites,
Tickling our noses in soft daylight fights.
While the monkeys swing with joyful grace,
They make it a challenge, a silly race!

With laughter echoing through the blue,
The world feels fresh, bright, and new.
So join the frolic, rise to the call,
In this canopy dance, let's laugh and fall!

Tranquil Horizons

As the sun dips low in hues of gold,
The horizon giggles, stories unfold.
A crab scuttles by with a sassy prance,
While waves join in, they too want to dance!

With drinks in hand and hats tilted wide,
We watch the antics of the ocean's tide.
The gulls make faces, a comic troupe,
We erupt with laughter, gathering the scoop!

In the twilight glow, shadows stretch long,
As we join the chorus, our silly song.
The breeze keeps whispering, "Join this fun!"
Running through thoughts as quick as a bun!

With joy we gather, under a moonlit sky,
Every giggle sounds like a sweet goodbye.
Forever in memory, these moments stay,
In tranquil horizons where laughter plays!

Through the Palms' Gaze

Through leafy frames, we watch the scene,
Where antics unfold, and smiles convene.
The wind teases hats, making them fly,
As we all break into a playful cry!

A little iguana strikes a pose,
On a sun-kissed rock, where laughter grows.
With every chuckle, the world feels light,
As we dance with shadows, hearts feeling bright!

The coconuts giggle as they roll free,
Each tumble a cheer; oh, what glee!
The palm fronds wave like pals in play,
Inviting us closer to join their ballet!

So let us toast to the silly delight,
As day turns to dusk, we hold on tight.
This mischievous moment, forever we'll praise,
Through the watchful palms, in their loving gaze!

Enchanted by the Coastal Rhythm

Beneath the sun, they dance and prance,
Each gentle breeze, a joyful chance.
They wiggle their leaves, they rock and roll,
Every gust a party for every soul.

A coconut drops, a surprising thud,
Leaving sunbathers buried in sand and mud.
The gulls are laughing, high in the sky,
As palm trees plot the next silly spy.

With hats made of fronds, they gather to gossip,
About the tourists who think they're a tropic.
They wink at the sun, a cheeky display,
As sunburned kids make sandcastles sway.

So come take a peek at this leafy crew,
Where laughter is fresh, and the humor's true.
In the coastal rhythm, they've found their groove,
In this dance of life, they joyfully move.

Tranquility Beneath the Canopy

Under the shade where moments freeze,
The palms tell stories in the gentle breeze.
With a rustling laugh, they share their tales,
Of fishing adventures and oceanic gales.

A lizard lounges, quite the lazy fella,
In meetings with fronds, he's the real big seller.
With a yawn and a stretch, he catches the rays,
While the palms gossip of long summer days.

They jive to the beat of the ocean's charm,
With a rhythm that feels just like a warm balm.
People stroll by with drinks in hand,
While the trees make bets on who'll trip on the sand.

As day turns to dusk and stars make their show,
The palm trees chuckle, excitement in tow.
In tranquility found where the breezes flow free,
They relish in moments of palm tree esprit.

Echoes of the Island's Heart

Whispers of joy in the island air,
Palms play a game of who's got the flair.
Leaves flap and twirl with delightful zest,
While tourists attempt some awkward quest.

Caught in a breeze, a hat takes off fast,
Sailing away, making memories last.
The palms all chuckle, shaking with glee,
At the sight of a sunhat dancing with spree.

They sing to the waves in a rhythmic tune,
As the bright sun dips, a costume party soon.
With shadows they cast, they create quite the show,
For peeking raccoons that adore to know.

Under twinkling stars, the laughter will rise,
And the palms will wink under starry skies.
With echoes of joy from their leafy domain,
They remind us that laughing is never in vain.

Sunlit Caresses in the Tropics

Brightly they shine in the golden light,
With fronds in a flutter, they steal our sight.
The waves serenade, creating a song,
While palm trees giggle, dancing along.

A tourist slips, just missing a fall,
And the palms erupt in a playful call.
With swaying hips and a cheeky cheer,
They invite all to join in the tropical sphere.

Sun-kissed moments wrapped in bright dreams,
Where nothing is awkward, or so it seems.
They sway with the rhythm of laughter and fun,
In the tropic's embrace, we all become one.

As dusk drapes down with a shimmering glow,
The palms wave goodnight, preparing to show
More shenanigans tomorrow, oh what a scene,
In the land of the palms where joy reigns supreme.

Whispering Canopy Tales

In the breeze, a dance so odd,
Leaves giggle like they just got a nod.
Fronds argue who gets the most sun,
While coconuts roll and have some fun.

Monkeys gossip in their leafy chair,
Plotting mischief without a care.
A toucan grins with a fruity beak,
And squirrels secretly seek a sneak peak.

The lizards boast of their bright attire,
As each one tries to climb a vine higher.
The shadows weave like a playful cat,
While crickets sing to a perky brat.

Under this roof, no worries remain,
Just silly tales in this leafy lane.
Laughing branches sway in delight,
As they sing to the stars each night.

Ocean's Resonance

Waves whisper secrets to the shore,
While shells giggle with an oceanic roar.
A starfish winks, and the seaweed twirls,
As the salty breeze teases the girls.

Seagulls squawk in a comical tune,
Trying to dance to the sun and the moon.
Jellyfish glide in a wobbly parade,
While fish try out their newest charade.

A crab with a top hat takes center stage,
As barnacles cheer, setting the gauge.
The ocean laughs in a bubbly spree,
Where every splash is a chorus, whee!

Each sunlit day is a salty delight,
With joyful antics sprinkled in bright.
In this playful field of frolic and flow,
The ocean's giggle is the star of the show.

Daydreams Beneath Palm Leaves

Beneath the greens, a carpet of bliss,
A lazy lizard steals a quick kiss.
Fronds tickle the air with a gentle tease,
While crickets sing symphonies with ease.

A snail makes its way with a determined heft,
Claiming the prize of an empty cleft.
Nearby, a butterfly dodges a breeze,
As grasshoppers giggle with unending tease.

The sun's warm glow creates shadows of glee,
As ants march in lines, planning their spree.
A lazy sloth shuffles with ample style,
As all in this grove pause for a while.

In this whimsical realm where laughter lives,
Nature hums tunes that each spirit gives.
Here's to the dreams in the rustling shade,
In a world where fun will never fade.

An Invitation from the Isles

Come hear the tales from the island's heart,
Where every coconut plays a part.
Parrots chuckle in colors so bright,
Calling all creatures to the dance tonight.

Turtles trot in their slow-motion strut,
As conch shells echo, a nature-filled rutt.
The hibiscus bloom with a wink and a grin,
While every sea breeze invites them in.

Lemurs hop with a jump and a flip,
Sipping nectar like it's a fine sip.
Under the moon, the grass shimmies and shakes,
Join in together for the fun that it makes.

So gather your friends and pack up a smile,
Come dance with us, if just for a while.
In this playful isle where the laughter is free,
Let the joyful vibes flow like the sea.

Rhythm of the Dunes

The sand huddles close, a dance so light,
Crabs pinch in rhythm, oh what a sight!
Seagulls all giggle, they can't seem to land,
As the wind whispers secrets, isn't life grand?

A flip-flop flies past, just out of reach,
As the sun's hot beams begin to teach.
Laughter erupts from our sandy abode,
With a tide that blushes, it's a goofy load.

The ocean waves chuckle, tickling our toes,
While jellyfish jiggle in their squishy clothes.
An octopus winks, what a sight to behold,
In this sandy circus, the fun never gets old.

So let's dance with the breeze, forget our woes,
As the dunes giggle softly, nobody knows!
The rhythm of nature, like a mischievous sprite,
In this beachy ballroom, we twirl day and night.

Green Giants' Conversations

In sun-kissed meadows, the giants convene,
With trunks full of wisdom, and leaves so green.
They gossip of squirrels, and rabbits that hop,
Of acorns and pinecones, they just can't stop.

With a creak and a crack, they joke about growth,
One's been to a spa, the other to both!
"Stretching my branches keeps me so spry,"
Piped a tall cedar, "I think I might fly!"

Blades of grass chuckle at their leafy jokes,
As the breeze tickles laughter from these leafy blokes.
The daisies are rolling, the tulips in glee,
While the sun is their spotlight, now that's the key!

And as twilight falls, they share their last tales,
Of adventures with owls, and nighttime details.
Among all the whispers of night's gentle charms,
The green giants chuckle, safe in their arms.

Swaying Whispers

In a backyard wild, where laughter takes flight,
The whispers of joy twirl under moonlight.
Cats on the fence take a late-night stroll,
Chasing shadows, living the extrovert role.

A picnic blanket hosts a bizarre feast,
With ants doing the conga, not caring in the least.
The lemonade giggles, it's way too sweet,
As a rogue ice cube declares, "Now that's a treat!"

The stars peek through, wearing sparkles like bling,
While crickets provide the most unexpected swing.
The owls hoot softly, joining the fun,
Under a sky where no worries outrun.

So let's raise our cups to the night's silly tune,
To all the wild dances beneath a big moon.
In a world full of whispers, let laughter take flight,
With frolicsome echoes carrying into the night.

Breezy Conversations

In the park full of laughter, oh what a scene,
The wind starts to chatter with leaves so green.
"Did you hear the one about the old oak?"
"He's got branches for arms and a trunk made of jokes!"

The flowers all giggle as they trade petal tales,
Of bees' buzzing antics and their silly trails.
A butterfly flutters, pretending to glide,
While squirrels play tag, no reason to hide.

A gust interrupts, with a whoosh and a cheer,
"Your petals are pretty, but watch out for beer!"
The daisies all snicker, holding their sway,
As the sun chuckles softly, lighting the way.

So here in this haven, where fun doesn't cease,
The breeze keeps on chatting, giving us peace.
Let's laugh with the flowers and spin with the air,
For every silly moment is one we should share.

Dance under the Stars

Beneath the twinkling light, we prance,
With limbs like noodles, we take a chance.
The rhythm's wild, we laugh and spin,
Falling over, where do we begin?

Feet so clumsy, we trip on air,
A chorus of laughs, without a care.
Stars watching closely, they wink and glow,
As we bust moves only we know.

The moon chuckles, a silver tease,
While we twirl round like cheeky bees.
We dance like penguins, it's quite absurd,
Yet every moment is blissfully heard.

As nights drift on in joyous delight,
Our laughter echoes, a funny sight.
With stardust on toes and giggles galore,
We leap and twirl till we can't anymore.

Coastal Embrace

The beach is our stage, the waves our beat,
With sunscreen splattered, oh what a feat!
My hat flies off; that's just my style,
Chasing it down with a goofy smile.

Seagulls squawk as they dive for fries,
While we juggle drinks under sunny skies.
Sand gets in places we can't confess,
Laughter erupts as we try to dress.

Our toes dance on grains, ticklish and bold,
While sunscreen stories are often retold.
With ice cream madness—a tasty miss,
We share a giggle, a sun-soaked bliss.

As the sun dips low with a golden glance,
We dance in the waves, gave it a chance.
Coastal breezes tug and tease at our clothes,
Making us twirl like no one knows.

Secrets of Sunlit Breezes

Breezes whisper secrets, cheeky and bright,
Tickling our noses in pure sunlight.
A gust comes in wearing shades so cool,
As we follow along like silly fools.

Tanned lobster legs dancing under the sun,
And laughter erupts as the breeze has fun.
With every twist, the hats take flight,
Chasing them down is quite the sight!

Our sunscreen debates turn wildly absurd,
With splatters and splashes like no one's heard.
Yet secrets are shared as we revel and sway,
With giggles and twists on this sunny day.

The breeze winks at us, like a playful friend,
Encouraging laughter, never to end.
Under bright rays, with antics so free,
We dance with the whispers of glee and spree.

Conversations with the Wind

The wind has opinions, oh what a chat,
"Let's flip this hat" it squeals with a spat.
Fluttering petals, they join in our fun,
As we argue with nature, all under the sun.

"Can you do this?" I challenge a breeze,
It tickles my neck like an itch that won't ease.
With a swirl and a swirl, it answers with glee,
"Try and catch me if you think you can see!"

Our laughter rises with each playful gust,
Sharing secrets of summer, it's truly a must.
We spin in a tango, a whimsical duel,
With the wind as our partner, it makes us feel cool.

As shadows grow long, and the skies turn to pink,
One last flip of laughter—a moment to think.
With breezy conversations beneath the vast skies,
We join in the dance where the humor never dies.

Coastal Echoes

A coconut fell with a thump,
I thought it was a monkey's jump.
The seagulls squawk like they own the road,
I swear they're planning a feathered code.

Beach balls bounce in a joyful spree,
Chasing crabs—oh, what a sight to see!
Sandcastles rise, but then they fall,
As laughter echoes, we make quite the call.

Flip-flops flying, oh what a race,
The sunburned tourists, all in one place.
Don't mind the sunburn; just take a chance,
As the waves invite us to join the dance.

With ice cream cones that melt away,
We chase the tide, what a foolish play!
Under the sun, all worries fade,
In this silly rhythm, our hearts are made.

Whispers from the Ocean

The tide whispered secrets to the shore,
But all I heard was the seagull's roar.
Flip-flops scattered, toes in the sand,
Oops! There goes my drink, it was unplanned.

Crabs do the cha-cha, what a bizarre sight,
Dancing in circles, under the moonlight.
I tried to join, but tripped on my own toe,
Now my dance moves really steal the show.

Seashells collect stories, the ocean's own lore,
I'm still looking for one that shows me the score.
With every wave crashing, I giggle and grin,
Who knew that laughter was my best fin?

The wind tousles hair, it's a playful tease,
A napkin flew off, catching a light breeze.
As I chase my sandwich that's up in the sky,
I realize that fun is just giving it a try.

A Tropical Reverie

In a hammock swung high by a lazy strand,
I pondered the secrets of this sunny land.
An orange drink spilled, oh spills are the best,
As ice cubes pirouette like they're on a quest.

Fruits pile high in a fruity parade,
Pineapples chuckle, refusing to fade.
The mango, a jester, laughs with a wink,
Making all the tourists stop and think.

Belly flops echo, a splash and a cheer,
As children run wild, no sign of fear.
Sand angels are made with careless delight,
In the sun's warm embrace, everything feels right.

Here comes a crab, marching like a king,
Stealing my sandwich, oh, what a thing!
Yet I just laugh at this silly charade,
In the game of beach life, we've all got it made.

Lifting Spirits on Soft Breezes

With a refreshing drink in hand, I feel bold,
The sun shines high, but the stories unfold.
A splash from a wave sent my hat on a fly,
Now a fish rushes by, like, 'Hey! Look at I!'

Seagulls argue o'er who gets the next fry,
While umbrellas flirt, under the bright sky.
Loud laughter rings as beach games commence,
Who knew that sand would hold such suspense?

A parrot squawks jokes, with a colorful flair,
While beachgoers clap and toss up their hair.
Each wave that rolls in brings a silly surprise,
Under sunswept skies, laughter never dies.

The sun begins setting with a glorious paint,
As I dodge a baby who's covered in pink paint.
With the night coming on, we toast to this bliss,
In the dance of the beach, who could ever miss?

Silhouettes at Twilight

Twilight's dance with shadows near,
A funky party, oh so clear.
Branches swing, a groovy beat,
Watch them move, oh what a treat!

Dancing shoes of nature's wear,
Breeze kicks up with wild flair.
Frolicking leaves in a silly twirl,
All around, they give a whirl!

Coconuts join in the fun,
Rolling 'round, they're never done.
They slip and slide, oh what a joke,
As laughter echoes, hearts provoke!

Underneath the starry glow,
Plant life shimmies, putting on a show.
Twilight brings a jig so bright,
Who knew trees could dance all night!

Nature's Gentle Sway

In the garden of verdant delight,
Plants prance around, oh what a sight!
A leafy jig that steals the show,
Who knew nature liked to flow?

With every gust, a leafy cheer,
A frond ballet that we all revere.
Branches bob, but don't break free,
Nature's humor, oh so carefree!

Butterflies join this festive spree,
Twisting and turning, as wild can be.
A riot of colors in the air,
An open dance floor laid bare!

Even the grass starts to twirl,
Their tiny moves can make you whirl.
With giggles spread on summer's stage,
Nature's got us all in a playful rage!

Windswept Dreams

Dreams take flight on breezy wings,
With nature's laughter, joy it brings.
The leaves discuss their latest fling,
In whispered winds, their secrets sing.

Bouncing branches, twist and shout,
While squirrels watch and look about.
They chat in nutty tones, you see,
About the best leaves for their tea!

The breeze invites a playful chase,
While clouds drift by in a hazy race.
A feathered friend joins in the fun,
With silly giggles under the sun!

As shadows grow longer, so do the laughs,
Nature's stand-up, with silly gaffes.
Rolling hills giggle, oh what a theme,
Life is a joke, or so it seems!

Under the Watchful Fronds

Underneath the leafy might,
Fronds on guard, ready for the night.
They gossip about the sun's last beam,
While crickets chirp in a rhythmic dream.

A sleepy lizard takes a leap,
Tangled up, he makes a heap.
The fronds just giggle, what a sight,
Nature's prankster, full of light!

Mice join in with tap dance feet,
Barely noticed, but oh so sweet.
While shadows sway, not a care,
Our leafy friends just laugh and stare!

As dusk paints the world a dark hue,
The chuckles linger, bold and true.
Life's a riot, under the trees,
Where laughter flutters on the breeze!

Song of the Tropics

In the sun, they dance and twirl,
With fronds that wave, they give a whirl.
They tickle the clouds with silly bends,
And whisper secrets to their leafy friends.

A squirrel swings by, catching the vibe,
He thinks he's slick, doing his jibe.
These trees are such jokers, in bright green gowns,
Even the coconuts giggle in towns.

A chirp from the birds adds to the play,
As they join the fun in their own little way.
With shadows that stretch like silly jokes,
The ground shakes with laughter, as sunlight pokes.

So here we groove in tropical sway,
With trees acting funny, come join the fray!
In the breeze, we grin with delight,
Life's a comedy, both day and night.

Breezes and Echoes

When the wind starts to tickle the leaves,
It sings a song that no one believes.
The branches chuckle and wiggle around,
Making odd shapes, they're a sight profound.

A parrot squawks with a silly pride,
While critters all gather, nowhere to hide.
Each gust that blows makes them dance and sway,
Like a wild party that's here to stay.

The shadows play tricks on sunbaked ground,
Jumping through laughter, in mirth they are found.
Echoes of joy bounce off the seas,
As every branch sways with such carefree ease.

So come take a laugh with nature's jest,
In the laughter of breezes, we're truly blessed!
In tropical rhythms, we frolic and cheer,
With echoes of fun ringing loud and clear.

The Dance of Nature's Giants

Oh, watch the big trunks with their funny stance,
In the tropical sun, they do a dance!
With arms outstretched, they twist and shout,
Waving to the sky, they'll never doubt.

The roots have rhythm, a beat so bold,
While lizards groove, like stars of gold.
Each leaf a partner, in a wacky spin,
Joining the fun, where the laughter begins!

Moody clouds grumble, might join in too,
As they drift around, painting skies blue.
The sun just chuckles, a bright yellow ray,
Watching large dancers in their playful display.

With the rhythm of nature, join the throng,
As we all sway to this quirky song!
In the heart of the tropics, we sing and sway,
With those giants of joy lighting our way.

Horizon's Embrace

Under a sky with patterns so funny,
The trees stretch wide, like a drink of honey.
Feeling the laughter in each gentle breeze,
While the sun peeks in, through giggling leaves.

The coastlines bounce like kites in the air,
While surfers glide without a care.
Driftwood cheers as the tide does its dance,
Nature's beauty in a whimsical trance.

Oh, those salty mists and teasing tries,
As the blue horizon plays peekaboo skies.
The tide's ticklish touch brings everyone near,
With a chorus of joy, and cheerful cheer.

So let's raise a drink and toast to the fun!
In this vibrant place, where the laughter's spun.
Embrace the horizon, wild and free,
In this silly dance, come sway with me!

Driftwood Dreams

In sandy shoes, I dance around,
A crab in shades, my friend is found.
He scuttles by, quite chic and spry,
Shells snapping selfies, oh my my!

A flip-flop lands upon my face,
A fish jumps high, a real disgrace.
I laugh and cheer, what a great show,
A beachside circus, don't you know?

My drink, a splash, with tiny straw,
A coconut's grin, can you see its awe?
Twirling umbrellas for all to see,
The party's here; it's just for me!

With driftwood tales and sun-kissed dream,
I'll make a sandman, how he'll beam.
The tide comes in, oh what a tease,
Life's a contest; who will freeze?

Tropical Twilight

As daylight fades, the shadows play,
Banana peels slip, what a way!
I trip and tumble, land in sand,
While parrots mock, how very grand!

A sunset drink, with a twist and a swirl,
Coconut hats for each girl and girl.
The howl of monkeys sets the night,
As stars come out, oh, what a sight!

I challenge a squirrel, who's braver in flight,
He steals my snack, oh what a fright!
With palm fronds clapping, hear their cheer,
A nightly festival, oh dear, oh dear!

Tropical giggles fill the air,
With each small hiccup, we cast our care.
Under the moon, we spin and sway,
In punchline paradise, come play, come play!

The Palmistry of Nature

I consult the leaves, a wise old palm,
He says, "Relax! Just breathe in calm."
But then a gust, sends my hat on a ride,
Chasing it down turns into a slide!

A breeze that tickles, a duck in disguise,
Waddling past with its curious eyes.
Pineapple squawks from a nearby vendor,
"Grab one quick; explore the splendor!"

The trees conspire, they all agree,
Laughter echoes; we're wild and free.
A snake in shorts joins for the fun,
As I throw confetti, there's more to come!

Life's twists and turns, a playful art,
Every misstep is part of the heart.
So let the palms give their best advice,
In this wild party, we roll like dice!

Gentle Caress of the Breeze

A gentle push from nature's hand,
Kites fly high, like dreams unplanned.
With each flutter, the laughter soars,
As seagulls swoop, they're great explorers!

My drink's umbrella, a little shy,
Keeps dodging raindrops from the sky.
While turtles shuffle with such grace,
In a shell race, towards first place!

The sun dips low, a splash of bright,
Mermaids sing, 'Stay out tonight!'
With flip-flops flung, and hair windswept,
We're dancing fools, the world's inept!

Oh, the breeze tickles, wraps around,
A whisper of fun in every sound.
As stars begin to twinkle and tease,
Life's a joke, a great breeze, a breeze!

Whispers of the Tropics' Soul

In the sun, the leaves do prance,
They wiggle and shake, it's quite a dance.
A coconut drops with a comic thud,
And birds laugh out loud in the warm, bright flood.

Beneath them, tourists take a nap,
Dreaming of food—like a giant fruit map.
But the breeze steals their hats and plays coy,
While the squirrels plot mischief—oh what joy!

A hammock swings wildly, a ride gone wrong,
Entangled in laughter, the sun sings a song.
The palms high-five each other in bliss,
As the clouds float by, a soft, fluffy kiss.

The whole tropical vibe is one big jest,
Where nature's punchlines are simply the best.
So raise your drink, let the humor unfold,
In this paradise, laughter is gold.

The Poetry of Windborne Leaves

A leaf flutters down with a soft little giggle,
While the breeze makes the branches just wiggle.
The sun beams laughter, the shadows for fun,
Where every hot moment feels like a pun.

Time flows like syrup, sticky and sweet,
The beach ball escapes, oh what a treat!
The children chase after, squeals fill the air,
As a crab in a top hat shows off his flair.

The whispers of nature, they tickle your ears,
As the sea sings a song to quell all your fears.
A palm leaf sneezes—achoo! What a shock!
And there goes the fruit roll, right off of the block!

With laughter as bright as the sunlight above,
This world is a canvas of joy and of love.
So grab a good chair, kick back, don't be tame,
For humor is nature's wild, wicked game.

Breeze Whispers through Canopies

A zephyr zoomed past with a cheeky grin,
It rustled the leaves, let the fun times begin!
The shadows are dancing, a comic parade,
As everyone's sunscreen just starts to fade.

A toucan drops in, with colors so bright,
Cracking jokes with a wiggle, what a sight!
The wind chimes in, making all things hum,
While the picnic ants march, like here they come!

The hammock's having a swing-off today,
With all the lizards joining the fray.
As coconuts tumble with splats on the shore,
The waves laugh and roll—who could ask for more?

So join this madcap, the tropical spree,
Where the breeze is a joke, light as can be.
When the rhythm of laughter is sweet and profound,
Nature knows how to turn life around.

Dance of the Fronds

There's a party tonight in the palm treetops,
Where fronds wave in time, like a dance that just hops.
A gust throws a party, and all of them sway,
As the sun starts to set, turning gold into gray.

The monkeys swing by, tails tangled and neat,
Making a ruckus, with moves that can't be beat.
"Hey, pass the bananas!" they screech and they squeal,
While the iguanas just chuckle—oh, what a deal!

The breeze hums a tune, it's a boisterous jig,
Every leaf's twirling, even the twig!
Clouds clap together, the sky's in a fit,
As laughter erupts, who could take a hint?

So join in the chaos, let the wind take you high,
As the palms play their music, beneath the blue sky.
With giggles and wiggly fun all around,
Life's a grand circus when joy is the sound.

Tropical Serenade

In the breeze, they dance around,
With floppy hats and roots unbound.
Their laughter swells, a rustling cheer,
While crabs scuttle near, wiggling in fear.

A flip-flop slides, a rescue quest,
As coconuts roll, they laugh the best.
The sun-baked joke floats on a wave,
Will someone save that untamed brave?

Unruly shadows, a comical show,
Bending low, then bursting to grow.
A topsy-turvy fashion craze,
With leaves as hats—we're in a daze!

Spraying juice on the unsuspecting,
The old coconut's quite the thing!
While gulls roll their eyes, a raucous hoop,
We all join in, a laughter-filled troupe.

A Melody in the Wind

The breeze has a song, a silly tune,
As palm fronds join the afternoon.
They shake their heads as if to say,
'Come dance with us and forget the day!'

A chicken struts with no shame at all,
Pecking snacks, making a scene at the mall.
The palm trees chuckle, a rustle of glee,
While seashells gossip beneath the sea.

With fronds flat and arms held wide,
As if to fit in, how hard they tried!
They joke about the sun's hot kiss,
Who wore the best tan? Oh, pure bliss!

Sandcastles rise in lopsided glee,
A royal court of sand, can you see?
The palm trees giggle, they can't keep still,
In their leafy realm, they rule with a thrill!

Secrets of the Shoreline

Underneath the sunny skies,
A turtle whispers, oh what lies!
The palms eavesdrop, their tops in a twist,
Giggling leaves can't resist!

A fish wearing glasses swims by with flair,
Saying, 'Dude, it's a wild fish affair!'
The palms are shaking, can't hold their mirth,
As crabs join in the hilarious birth.

Surfboards tumble, catching a wave,
Palm fronds clapping like they're brave.
'Come on, you can do it!' they call out loud,
As dolphins leap, they cheer like a crowd.

A secret dance beneath the sun,
Where sea and trees play and run.
They giggle and chime, no need to be shy,
The shoreline sings, oh my, oh my!